OBJECTS

# Discovering
# Prisms

## Nancy Furstinger
## and John Willis

MEDIA ENHANCED BOOKS
AV2 BY WEIGL™
ADDED VALUE • AUDIO VISUAL

www.av2books.com

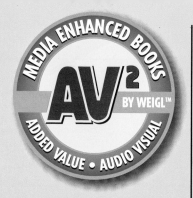

AV² provides enriched content that supplements and complements this book. Weigl's AV² books strive to create inspired learning and engage young minds in a total learning experience.

## Your AV² Media Enhanced books come alive with...

**Audio**
Listen to sections of the book read aloud.

**Key Words**
Study vocabulary, and complete a matching word activity.

**Video**
Watch informative video clips.

**Quizzes**
Test your knowledge.

**Embedded Weblinks**
Gain additional information for research.

**Slide Show**
View images and captions, and prepare a presentation.

**Try This!**
Complete activities and hands-on experiments.

**... and much, much more!**

Go to www.av2books.com, and enter this book's unique code.

### BOOK CODE

**E 3 6 4 7 2 5**

AV² by Weigl brings you media enhanced books that support active learning.

Published by AV² by Weigl
350 5ᵗʰ Avenue, 59ᵗʰ Floor
New York, NY 10118
www.av2books.com

Copyright © 2017 AV² by Weigl

Library of Congress Cataloging-in-Publication Data

Names: Furstinger, Nancy, author. | Willis, John, 1989-, author.
Title: Discovering prisms / Nancy Furstinger and John Willis.
Description: New York, NY : AV2 by Weigl, [2017] | Series: 3D objects |
  Includes bibliographical references and index.
Identifiers: LCCN 2016005657| ISBN 9781489649775 (hard cover : alk. paper) |
  ISBN 9781489649782 (soft cover : alk. paper) | ISBN 9781489649799 (Multi-user ebk.)
Subjects: LCSH: Prisms--Juvenile literature. | Diffraction--Juvenile
  literature. | Light--Properties--Juvenile literature.
Classification: LCC QA491 .F87 2017 | DDC 535/.420284--dc23
LC record available at http://lccn.loc.gov/2016005657

Printed in the United States of America in Brainerd, Minnesota
1 2 3 4 5 6 7 8 9 0  20 19 18 17 16

082016
210716

Project Coordinator: John Willis    Art Director: Terry Paulhus

# CONTENTS

# MAKING RAINBOWS

In science class, the teacher passes out glass **prisms**. She says that you can use the three-sided shapes to make rainbows indoors.

You hold your glass prism up to the sunlight. Against the opposite wall, you can see a rainbow of colors, red, orange, yellow, green, blue, and violet. Your teacher says that white light is made of many colors. When it passes through the prism, it separates into the colors of the rainbow.

Clear, see-through objects that separate white light into a rainbow are called "optical prisms." Optical prisms do not have to be prism-shaped.

In art class, you fold a piece of paper into thirds. You write your name on it and decorate it. Now you have a nameplate for your desk. Did you notice how the shape of the glass prism matches the shape of the nameplate? Both of these shapes are prisms.

Even some foods are shaped like prisms.

# WHAT DOES A PRISM LOOK LIKE?

Prisms are everywhere around us. Prisms are not flat. They have three **dimensions**. Shapes with only two dimensions, like a triangle, are flat. These flat shapes are also called **plane** shapes or 2D shapes. They have length and width.

Shapes such as prisms that have three dimensions are called **3D** shapes. Prisms have three dimensions people can measure. These are length, width, and height. 3D shapes are also called solid shapes.

How can we identify a prism? Look closely. A prism has a top, bottom, and sides, called **faces**. These faces are two-dimensional flat **surfaces**. Each face forms a surface of a 3D shape.

Many toys are shaped like prisms.

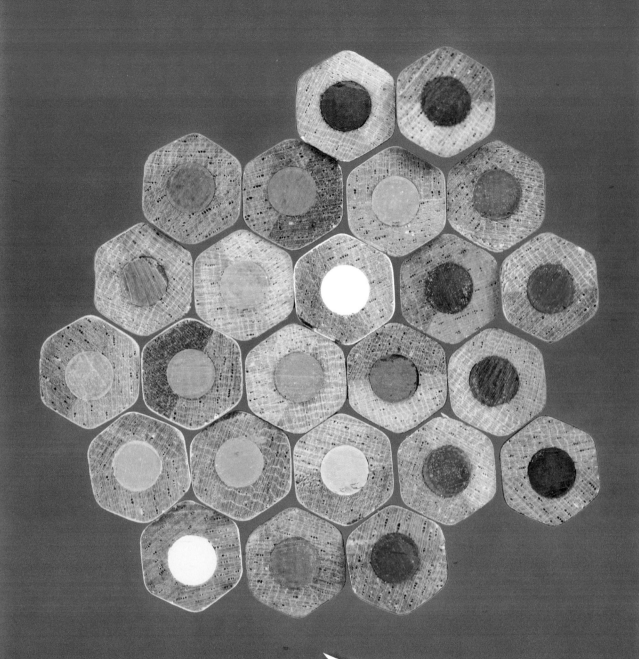

An unsharpened pencil is prism-shaped. Its two ends are the same shape.

# HOW DO WE KNOW IF A SHAPE IS A PRISM?

The ends of a prism have two faces that match. Different types of prisms have different shapes. Each prism is named for the shape of its ends, or **base**.

A prism's base can be a triangle, a rectangle, or a square. The base can even be a pentagon with five sides, a hexagon with six sides, or an octagon with eight sides. The two bases of a prism are always identical. They are exactly the same shape and size. The bases are **parallel**, too.

The number of sides depends upon the shape of the prism. A triangular prism has three sides. A rectangular prism has four sides. A pentagonal prism has five sides. A hexagonal prism has six sides. An octagonal prism has eight sides.

# PARTS OF A PRISM

side

The base of a prism can come in several different shapes.

base

# PRISMS AND TRIANGLES

Now that you know what a prism looks like, you can easily find this 3D shape. You will start seeing prisms in everyday objects.

It is summertime, and your family hikes along your favorite forest trail. You find the perfect campsite. It is flat and near the lake. Time to set up your roomy tent. First, pound in your tent stakes. Then, assemble the poles. Finally, put up your tent.

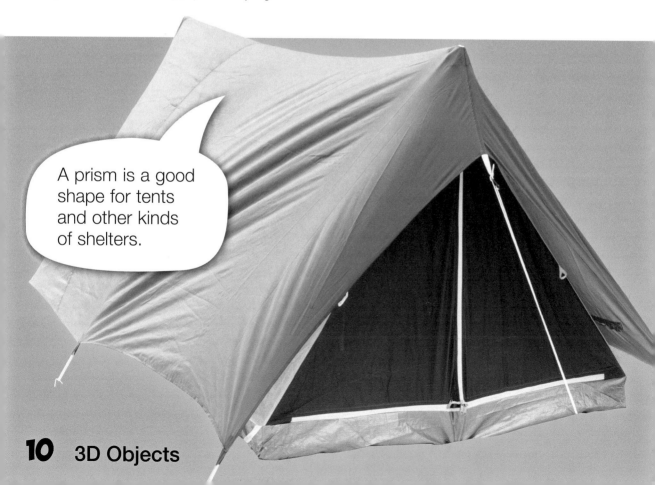

A prism is a good shape for tents and other kinds of shelters.

You hike past cabins in the woods. These A-frame houses are shaped like a big letter A. This shape allows heavy snow to slide off the roof and down to the ground. Back home, you set up a tent frame in your bedroom. Cover it with a quilt and fill it with pillows. Now you have a special hideaway to enjoy.

Did you notice all of these places are shaped like triangular prisms? They have bases that are triangles. The other three sides are rectangles.

Prism-shaped houses with pointy roofs are less likely to be damaged by heavy snow or lots of rain.

# PRISMS AND RECTANGLES

Today is your teacher's birthday. You bake her a big batch of brownies. Then, you carefully layer them in a box. You hope your teacher will share the brownies with your class.

Someone in your class gives your teacher a new lunchbox. Another student brings juice boxes. The juice goes great with the brownies.

The principal brings your teacher a dictionary. After school, the janitor arrives with a box of chalk and a new eraser.

Did you notice that all of the presents are shaped like rectangular prisms? They have two bases and four faces that are all rectangles.

Even lunchboxes can be prism-shaped.

# PRISMS AND CUBES

Your little brother cranks the handle of his jack-in-the-box. The song "Pop Goes the Weasel" plays. Suddenly, a clown pops out of the box.

You pull a board game off the shelf. Shake the dice and roll them. Who can race around the board first? Later, you take out a set of alphabet blocks and help your brother spell words.

Did you know that another 3D shape is a special type of rectangular prism? This shape is called a **cube**. The cube has six equal faces. Each face is an identical square. Look closely at your brother's toys. They are all cubes.

Dice have been around for many years. Ancient Egyptians used them more than 4,000 years ago.

# MANY-SIDED PRISMS

When your family stops for a yard sale, you search for prisms. That crystal paperweight could be a prism. You closely examine it. The paperweight has five sides, so it is a pentagonal prism.

Next, you find a box of yellow pencils. Take a new pencil out of the box and count its sides. There are six, so the pencil is a hexagonal prism.

Once a pencil is sharpened, it is no longer a prism. It loses one of its two hexagonal faces.

You spot a splendid music box. When you open the lid, a song starts playing. This box looks old and beautiful. As you bring the box to your mother, count the sides. There are six, so the box is a hexagonal prism.

The first music box was made in Switzerland in the early 1800s.

# BEES AND PRISMS

Smart bees build their honeycombs using prisms that have six sides. Look closely at a honeycomb. Every cell is shaped like a hexagon. All of these shapes fit together like a jigsaw puzzle.

Have you ever wondered why bees use this shape? The hexagon requires less beeswax to build than other shapes. Keep in mind that it takes eight ounces of honey to make one ounce of beeswax. With a hexagon shape, bees do not have to work as hard.

When the honeycomb is finished, it holds more honey than if the bees used other shapes. No wonder a hive full of honey is so heavy.

Honey bees use honeycomb to store their honey. They need this extra honey during the winter, when there are fewer flowers.

# COPYING THE HONEYCOMB DESIGN

People often look to nature for ideas. When inventors realized how smart the honeycomb shape is, they got to work. Now, there are many products using this strong and lightweight hexagon. Hexagons can be found in airplanes, trains, and buildings.

Hexagonal designs are also stronger than many other shapes.

# CRYSTAL PRISMS AND GIANT PRISMS

You can find more prism shapes in nature. Sometimes, **crystals** and rocks form prism shapes.

Garnets are beautiful gems. They come in almost every color of the rainbow, especially reds and greens. The garnet is the state gemstone of New York. Many garnets form as prisms.

Quartz is one of the most common minerals on Earth.

Some rocks are huge prisms. The Giant's Causeway is in Northern Ireland. These pillars of stone are made from basalt rock. An ancient story says they formed in a fight between two giants.

Search for prism shapes in your house and everywhere you go. You will be amazed how many of these 3D shapes you can find.

The Giant's Causeway is made up of about 40,000 pillars of basalt.

# PRISM QUIZ

1. How many sides does an octagon have?

2. Are all optical prisms prism-shaped?

3. What two colors are often seen in garnets?

4. What kind of prism is an unsharpened pencil?

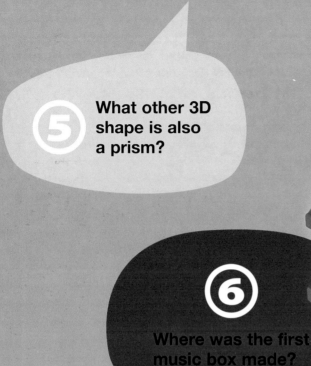

**5** What other 3D shape is also a prism?

**6** Where was the first music box made?

**7** Who used dice more than 4,000 years ago?

**8** Why do bees use hexagon shapes when making honeycombs?

Answers:
1. Eight  2. No  3. Red and green  4. A hexagonal prism  5. A cube  6. Switzerland  7. Ancient Egyptians  8. They require less beeswax to build than other shapes

# ACTIVITY:
## PRISM POSTERS

Use this poster to display different shapes of prisms.

### Materials

- magazines
- poster board
- scissors
- glue stick
- markers

### Directions

1. Search in magazines for real-life examples of prisms. Cut out the photographs that you find.

2. Arrange the photographs by what type of base the prism has. Remember, prisms can have a base that is a triangle, rectangle, square, pentagon, hexagon, or octagon.

3. When you are happy with your arrangement, glue the photographs to the poster board. Let the glue dry.

4. Write captions telling what types of prism your photographs show. Display your poster.

# KEY WORDS

**3D:** a shape with length, width, and height

**base:** a flat surface on a 3D shape

**crystals:** a transparent mineral, such as quartz

**cube:** a 3D shape with six equal, square sides

**dimensions:** the length, width, or height of an object

**faces:** flat surfaces on a 3D shape

**parallel:** lines that are always the same distance apart

**plane:** a flat surface

**prisms:** 3D shapes with bases that are identical shapes and sides that are parallel

**surfaces:** the flat or curved borders of a 3D shape

# INDEX

# Log on to www.av2books.com

AV² by Weigl brings you media enhanced books that support active learning. Go to www.av2books.com, and enter the special code found on page 2 of this book. You will gain access to enriched and enhanced content that supplements and complements this book. Content includes video, audio, weblinks, quizzes, a slide show, and activities.

## AV² Online Navigation

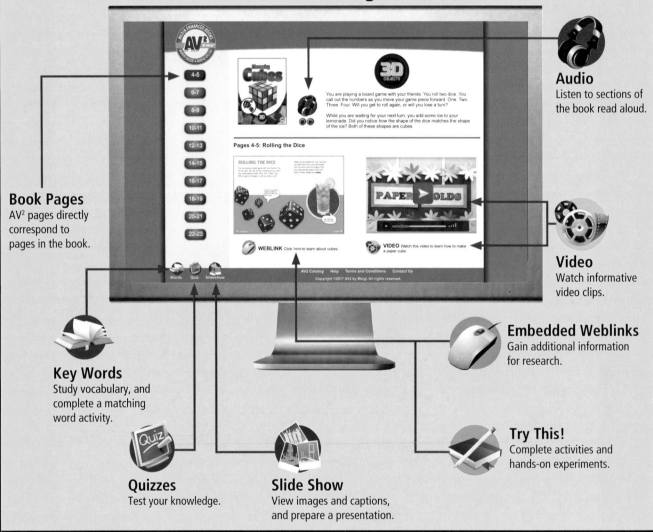

**Audio**
Listen to sections of the book read aloud.

**Video**
Watch informative video clips.

**Book Pages**
AV² pages directly correspond to pages in the book.

**Key Words**
Study vocabulary, and complete a matching word activity.

**Quizzes**
Test your knowledge.

**Slide Show**
View images and captions, and prepare a presentation.

**Embedded Weblinks**
Gain additional information for research.

**Try This!**
Complete activities and hands-on experiments.

---

AV² was built to bridge the gap between print and digital. We encourage you to tell us what you like and what you want to see in the future.

## Sign up to be an AV² Ambassador at www.av2books.com/ambassador.